When life feels good, when
life feels bad - A journal
to express your feelings

YIN YANG
Journal

ISBN-13: 978-1720457398
ISBN-10: 1720457395

Published in July 2018 by Plum Design & Publishing Ltd
www.plumdesignpublishing.com
Based in Berkshire, UK

Other series and titles available:

- Love Journal
- Daily Success Journal
- Gratitude Journal Butterfly (available in 7 vibrant colours)
- Gratitude at Home Series including:
    - A parent's book 'Gratitude at Home'
    - Gratitude Journals ranging from age 2 to 20
- Gratitude in Schools Series including:
    - Teacher's guide 'Gratitude in Primary Schools'
    - Teacher's guide 'Gratitude in Secondary Schools
      and Further Education'
    - Gratitude Journals ranging from age 5 to 20

To find out more, visit **www.inspiringjournals.com**

The principles of Yin and Yang

"Yin and yang, male and female, strong and weak, rigid and tender, heaven and earth, light and darkness, thunder and lightning, cold and warmth, good and evil... the interplay of opposite principles constitutes the universe."
Confucius

If you are not so familiar with the meaning of Yin and Yang, it's a Chinese symbol representing the balance in life. Wikipedia describes it best:

"In Chinese philosophy, yin and yang (lit. 'dark-bright', 'negative-positive') describes how seemingly opposite or contrary forces may actually be complementary, interconnected, and interdependent in the natural world, and how they may give rise to each other as they interrelate to one another. Many tangible dualities (such as light and dark, fire and water, expanding and contracting) are thought of as physical manifestations of the duality symbolised by yin and yang."

The Yin is the dark swirl and the Yang is the light swirl. They each contain a dot of the opposite colour, which gives the clue to the meaning of Yin and Yang, that everything contains the seed of its opposite.

Below are some examples of the meaning of both symbols and their opposites:

Yin (black swirl) -	Yang (white swirl) +
Negative charge	Positive charge
Female	Male
Dark/Moon	Light/Bright/Sun
Recessive/Nurturing	Strong/Assertive
Damp/Cool/Water	Dry/Hot/Fire
Earth	Heaven
Autumn & Winter	Spring & Summer
Sad/Weak	Happy/Strong
Still/Passive/Calm	Moving/Active/Energetic
Hard/Quiet	Soft/Loud

Introduction

The purpose of this Yin Yang journal is to help you on a day to day basis for the next 12 weeks. Life is not always straight forward and has its challenges, so it's good to get some of our negative thoughts and feelings down on paper, as well as the positives.

Don't let your challenges affect you. Good on you for recognising something wasn't right. Because you are doing it, you are working towards your future, and by writing it down, you can look back and watch yourself grow.

We all have a vision for our future. What does it look like for you? By putting it out there, you are sending a message out to the Universe expressing what you want.

As you grow on your journey, you'll look back and see how far you've come. You've got a great future ahead of you.

Be inspired. Do more personal growth. This journal is the first step on your growth journey. When you are ready for your next step, look at my Gratitude Journal Butterfly or my Daily Success Journal.

How to use your journal

At the beginning of your journal, fill in the page "Start Here" and answer all three questions. It will help you take stock of where you are at as you start using this journal. At the end of the journal, on the page "Finish Here", you'll get to reflect about your progress and journey of transformation.

For each day, there are two pages - the left page is for writing down the yins, which would be your challenges, negative thoughts or feelings. The right page is for writing down the yangs, which would be your achievements, positives thoughts or feelings.

If you need a bit of help getting in touch with your feelings, put your hand on your heart, close your eyes and ask yourself "How do I feel today?"

Please be honest but stay kind to yourself. Nowadays we tend to think too much and forget to feel. This is so important. It will make a big difference, so please do your best to do it.

There are free flow spaces in this journal: you can use these pages to write, draw or doodle. An idea could be to use them to create what your dream future would look like as you progress on your journey.

You will also find inspirational quotes relating to yin and yang/balance with some Chinese symbols. At the end of the journal, you'll find all the symbols used and their meaning and you'll be able to have fun practising drawing them!

Remember that what you give out to others with abundance, also give back to yourself. Do your best and be your best every day. That's all you can do. Live, love, appreciate and be kind to yourself.

Wishing you the fulfilling, happy and balanced life that you deserve.

With love and gratitude,
Chrystel ♥

. . . .

For more journals, for inspiration or to stay in touch:

W www.inspiringjournals.com   **𝓟** Chrystel Melhuish

f @inspiringjournals   **◙** chrystelmelhuish

𝕐 @plumdesignpub   **in** Chrystel Melhuish

Thank You Gift: Download your free eBook "The Power of Gratitude" and discover 20 simple strategies to transform your life through the amazing power of gratitude. Visit **www.inspiringjournals.com/gift**

START HERE...

BEGINNING OF MY JOURNALING JOURNEY

Date: ....

Answer the following questions:
1. Where am I NOW in my life?
2. How do I FEEL about it?
3. What does my VISION for my future look like NOW, as I start using this journal?

_____

_____

_____

_____

_____

_____

_____

_____

_____

_____

_____

_____

_____

Stars and the moon will always need the darkness to be seen, the darkness will just not be worth having without the moon and the stars.

C. JoyBell C.

FREE FLOW SPACE
(Use this page to write, draw or doodle)

Date _____

MY YINS

What was challenging about today?
How did it make me feel?

_____

_____

_____

_____

_____

What did I learn from it? What better choices would I make in the future? Who helped me?

_____

_____

_____

_____

How do I feel now that it's out of my mind and on paper?
(tick or colour in your chosen emotion and/or write it down)

_____

_____

That's great! **It's so important to acknowledge the negative, so you can release it and may learn from it.** Please move on to the yangs.

MY YANGS

What was positive about today?
What did I achieve? What made me happy?

_____

_____

_____

_____

_____

_____

_____

_____

_____

How did it make me feel?
(tick or colour in your chosen emotion and write about it)

😄   🙂   😊

_____

_____

_____

Excellent! **It's just as important to recognise all the positives so you can appreciate your life and see how lucky you are.** ⭐

Date _____

MY YINS

What was challenging about today?
How did it make me feel?

_____

_____

_____

_____

What did I learn from it? What better choices would I make in the future? Who helped me?

_____

_____

_____

How do I feel now that it's out of my mind and on paper?
(tick or colour in your chosen emotion and/or write it down)

_____

That's great! **It's so important to acknowledge the negative, so you can release it and may learn from it.** Please move on to the yangs.

MY YANGS

What was positive about today?
What did I achieve? What made me happy?

_____

_____

_____

_____

_____

_____

_____

_____

_____

How did it make me feel?
(tick or colour in your chosen emotion and write about it)

_____

_____

_____

_____

Excellent! **It's just as important to recognise all the positives so you can appreciate your life and see how lucky you are.** ⭐★

Date _____

MY YINS

What was challenging about today?
How did it make me feel?

_____

_____

_____

_____

_____

What did I learn from it? What better choices would I make in the future? Who helped me?

_____

_____

_____

_____

How do I feel now that it's out of my mind and on paper?
(tick or colour in your chosen emotion and/or write it down)

_____

That's great! **It's so important to acknowledge the negative, so you can release it and may learn from it.** Please move on to the yangs.

MY YANGS

What was positive about today?
What did I achieve? What made me happy?

_____

_____

_____

_____

_____

_____

_____

_____

_____

_____

How did it make me feel?
(tick or colour in your chosen emotion and write about it)

☺ ☺ ☺

_____

_____

_____

Excellent! **It's just as important to recognise all the positives so you can appreciate your life and see how lucky you are.** ★⁂

Date ....

MY YINS

What was challenging about today?
How did it make me feel?

What did I learn from it? What better choices would I make in the future? Who helped me?

How do I feel now that it's out of my mind and on paper?
(tick or colour in your chosen emotion and/or write it down)

That's great! **It's so important to acknowledge the negative, so you can release it and may learn from it.** Please move on to the yangs.

MY YANGS

What was positive about today?
What did I achieve? What made me happy?

How did it make me feel?
(tick or colour in your chosen emotion and write about it)

Excellent! **It's just as important to recognise all the positives so you can appreciate your life and see how lucky you are.** ★★

Date _____

MY YINS

What was challenging about today?
How did it make me feel?

_____

_____

_____

_____

What did I learn from it? What better choices would I make in the future? Who helped me?

_____

_____

_____

_____

How do I feel now that it's out of my mind and on paper?
(tick or colour in your chosen emotion and/or write it down)

_____

That's great! **It's so important to acknowledge the negative, so you can release it and may learn from it.** Please move on to the yangs.

MY YANGS

What was positive about today?
What did I achieve? What made me happy?

_____

_____

_____

_____

_____

_____

_____

_____

How did it make me feel?
(tick or colour in your chosen emotion and write about it)

☺ ☺ ☺

_____

_____

_____

Excellent! **It's just as important to recognise all the positives so you can appreciate your life and see how lucky you are.** ★★

Date _____

MY YINS

What was challenging about today?
How did it make me feel?

_____

_____

_____

_____

_____

What did I learn from it? What better choices would I make in the future? Who helped me?

_____

_____

_____

_____

How do I feel now that it's out of my mind and on paper?
(tick or colour in your chosen emotion and/or write it down)

_____

_____

That's great! **It's so important to acknowledge the negative, so you can release it and may learn from it.** Please move on to the yangs.

MY YANGS

What was positive about today?
What did I achieve? What made me happy?

_____

_____

_____

_____

_____

_____

_____

_____

How did it make me feel?
(tick or colour in your chosen emotion and write about it)

☺ ☺ ☺

_____

_____

_____

Excellent! **It's just as important to recognise all the positives so you can appreciate your life and see how lucky you are.** ★

Date _____

MY YINS

What was challenging about today?
How did it make me feel?

_____

_____

_____

_____

What did I learn from it? What better choices would I make in the future? Who helped me?

_____

_____

_____

_____

How do I feel now that it's out of my mind and on paper?
(tick or colour in your chosen emotion and/or write it down)

_____

_____

That's great! **It's so important to acknowledge the negative, so you can release it and may learn from it.** Please move on to the yangs.

MY YANGS

What was positive about today?
What did I achieve? What made me happy?

_____

_____

_____

_____

_____

_____

_____

_____

_____

_____

How did it make me feel?
(tick or colour in your chosen emotion and write about it)

_____

_____

_____

Excellent! **It's just as important to recognise all the positives so you can appreciate your life and see how lucky you are.** ⭐⭐

Accept your dark side,
understanding it will help
you to move with the light.
Knowing both sides of
our souls, helps us all
to move forward in life
and to understand that,
perfection doesn't exist.

Martin R. Lemieux

FREE FLOW SPACE
(Use this page to write, draw or doodle)

Date ....

MY YINS

What was challenging about today?
How did it make me feel?

....

....

....

....

....

What did I learn from it? What better choices would I make in the future? Who helped me?

....

....

....

....

How do I feel now that it's out of my mind and on paper?
(tick or colour in your chosen emotion and/or write it down)

....

....

That's great! **It's so important to acknowledge the negative, so you can release it and may learn from it.** Please move on to the yangs.

MY YANGS

What was positive about today?
What did I achieve? What made me happy?

_____

_____

_____

_____

_____

_____

_____

How did it make me feel?
(tick or colour in your chosen emotion and write about it)

_____

_____

_____

_____

Excellent! **It's just as important to recognise all the positives so you can appreciate your life and see how lucky you are.** ⭐

Date ....

MY YINS

What was challenging about today?
How did it make me feel?

_____

_____

_____

_____

What did I learn from it? What better choices would I make in the future? Who helped me?

_____

_____

_____

_____

How do I feel now that it's out of my mind and on paper?
(tick or colour in your chosen emotion and/or write it down)

_____

_____

That's great! **It's so important to acknowledge the negative, so you can release it and may learn from it.** Please move on to the yangs.

MY YANGS

What was positive about today?
What did I achieve? What made me happy?

_____

_____

_____

_____

_____

_____

_____

_____

How did it make me feel?
(tick or colour in your chosen emotion and write about it)

😄 🙂 🙂

_____

_____

_____

Excellent! **It's just as important to recognise all the positives so you can appreciate your life and see how lucky you are.** ⭐

Date _____

MY YINS

What was challenging about today?
How did it make me feel?

_____

_____

_____

_____

What did I learn from it? What better choices would I make in the future? Who helped me?

_____

_____

_____

_____

How do I feel now that it's out of my mind and on paper?
(tick or colour in your chosen emotion and/or write it down)

_____

_____

That's great! **It's so important to acknowledge the negative, so you can release it and may learn from it.** Please move on to the yangs.

MY YANGS

What was positive about today?
What did I achieve? What made me happy?

_____

_____

_____

_____

_____

_____

_____

_____

How did it make me feel?
(tick or colour in your chosen emotion and write about it)

😆 🙂 😊

_____

_____

_____

Excellent! It's just as important to recognise all the positives so you can appreciate your life and see how lucky you are. ★★

Date _____

MY YINS

What was challenging about today?
How did it make me feel?

_____

_____

_____

_____

_____

What did I learn from it? What better choices would I make in the future? Who helped me?

_____

_____

_____

_____

How do I feel now that it's out of my mind and on paper?
(tick or colour in your chosen emotion and/or write it down)

_____

_____

That's great! **It's so important to acknowledge the negative, so you can release it and may learn from it.** Please move on to the yangs.

MY YANGS

What was positive about today?
What did I achieve? What made me happy?

_____

_____

_____

_____

_____

_____

_____

_____

How did it make me feel?
(tick or colour in your chosen emotion and write about it)

_____

_____

_____

Excellent! **It's just as important to recognise all the positives so you can appreciate your life and see how lucky you are.** ⭐

MY YINS

What was challenging about today?
How did it make me feel?

What did I learn from it? What better choices would I make in the future? Who helped me?

How do I feel now that it's out of my mind and on paper?
(tick or colour in your chosen emotion and/or write it down)

That's great! **It's so important to acknowledge the negative, so you can release it and may learn from it.** Please move on to the yangs.

MY YANGS

What was positive about today?
What did I achieve? What made me happy?

_____

_____

_____

_____

_____

_____

_____

_____

How did it make me feel?
(tick or colour in your chosen emotion and write about it)

😄 🙂 😊

_____

_____

_____

Excellent! **It's just as important to recognise all the positives so you can appreciate your life and see how lucky you are.** ⭐⭐

Date _____

MY YINS

What was challenging about today?
How did it make me feel?

_____

_____

_____

_____

What did I learn from it? What better choices would I make in the future? Who helped me?

_____

_____

_____

_____

How do I feel now that it's out of my mind and on paper?
(tick or colour in your chosen emotion and/or write it down)

_____

That's great! **It's so important to acknowledge the negative, so you can release it and may learn from it.** Please move on to the yangs.

MY YANGS

What was positive about today?
What did I achieve? What made me happy?

_____

_____

_____

_____

_____

_____

_____

_____

How did it make me feel?
(tick or colour in your chosen emotion and write about it)

☺ ☺ ☺

_____

_____

_____

Excellent! **It's just as important to recognise all the positives so you can appreciate your life and see how lucky you are.** ⭐

Date _____

MY YINS

What was challenging about today?
How did it make me feel?

_____

_____

_____

_____

_____

What did I learn from it? What better choices would I make in the future? Who helped me?

_____

_____

_____

_____

How do I feel now that it's out of my mind and on paper?
(tick or colour in your chosen emotion and/or write it down)

_____

That's great! **It's so important to acknowledge the negative, so you can release it and may learn from it.** Please move on to the yangs.

MY YANGS

What was positive about today?
What did I achieve? What made me happy?

_____

_____

_____

_____

_____

_____

_____

_____

How did it make me feel?
(tick or colour in your chosen emotion and write about it)

😄 🙂 🙂

_____

_____

_____

Excellent! **It's just as important to recognise all the positives so you can appreciate your life and see how lucky you are.** ★

So it is said, for him who understands Heavenly joy, life is the working of Heaven; death is the transformation of things. In stillness, he and the yin share a single Virtue; in motion, he and the yang share a single flow.

Zhuangzi
The Complete Works of Chuang Tzu

FREE FLOW SPACE
(Use this page to write, draw or doodle)

Date ....

MY YINS

What was challenging about today?
How did it make me feel?

....

....

....

....

What did I learn from it? What better choices would I make
in the future? Who helped me?

....

....

....

....

How do I feel now that it's out of my mind and on paper?
(tick or colour in your chosen emotion and/or write it down)

....

....

That's great! **It's so important to acknowledge the negative, so you can release it and may learn from it.** Please move on to the yangs.

MY YANGS

What was positive about today?
What did I achieve? What made me happy?

_____

_____

_____

_____

_____

_____

_____

_____

_____

How did it make me feel?
(tick or colour in your chosen emotion and write about it)

😄 🙂 😊

_____

_____

_____

_____

Excellent! **It's just as important to recognise all the positives so you can appreciate your life and see how lucky you are.** ⭐

Date ....

MY YINS

What was challenging about today?
How did it make me feel?

....

....

....

....

....

What did I learn from it? What better choices would I make in the future? Who helped me?

....

....

....

....

How do I feel now that it's out of my mind and on paper?
(tick or colour in your chosen emotion and/or write it down)

That's great! **It's so important to acknowledge the negative, so you can release it and may learn from it.** Please move on to the yangs.

MY YANGS

What was positive about today?
What did I achieve? What made me happy?

How did it make me feel?
(tick or colour in your chosen emotion and write about it)

Excellent! **It's just as important to recognise all the positives so you can appreciate your life and see how lucky you are.** ⭐⭐

Date _____

MY YINS

What was challenging about today?
How did it make me feel?

_____

_____

_____

_____

_____

What did I learn from it? What better choices would I make in the future? Who helped me?

_____

_____

_____

_____

How do I feel now that it's out of my mind and on paper?
(tick or colour in your chosen emotion and/or write it down)

_____

_____

That's great! **It's so important to acknowledge the negative, so you can release it and may learn from it.** Please move on to the yangs.

MY YANGS

What was positive about today?
What did I achieve? What made me happy?

_____

_____

_____

_____

_____

_____

_____

_____

_____

How did it make me feel?
(tick or colour in your chosen emotion and write about it)

😄 🙂 🙂

_____

_____

_____

Excellent! **It's just as important to recognise all the positives so you can appreciate your life and see how lucky you are.** ★★

Date· ....

MY YINS

What was challenging about today?
How did it make me feel?

....

....

....

....

....

What did I learn from it? What better choices would I make in the future? Who helped me?

....

....

....

....

How do I feel now that it's out of my mind and on paper?
(tick or colour in your chosen emotion and/or write it down)

....

....

That's great! **It's so important to acknowledge the negative, so you can release it and may learn from it.** Please move on to the yangs.

MY YANGS

What was positive about today?
What did I achieve? What made me happy?

_____

_____

_____

_____

_____

_____

_____

_____

How did it make me feel?
(tick or colour in your chosen emotion and write about it)

☺ ☺ ☺

_____

_____

_____

Excellent! **It's just as important to recognise all the positives so you can appreciate your life and see how lucky you are.** ⭐

Date _____

MY YINS

What was challenging about today?
How did it make me feel?

_____

_____

_____

_____

What did I learn from it? What better choices would I make in the future? Who helped me?

_____

_____

_____

_____

How do I feel now that it's out of my mind and on paper?
(tick or colour in your chosen emotion and/or write it down)

_____

_____

That's great! **It's so important to acknowledge the negative, so you can release it and may learn from it.** Please move on to the yangs.

MY YANGS

What was positive about today?
What did I achieve? What made me happy?

_____

_____

_____

_____

_____

_____

_____

_____

_____

How did it make me feel?
(tick or colour in your chosen emotion and write about it)

☺ ☺ ☺

_____

_____

_____

Excellent! **It's just as important to recognise all the positives so you can appreciate your life and see how lucky you are.** ⭐⭐

Date _____

MY YINS

What was challenging about today?
How did it make me feel?

_____
_____
_____
_____

What did I learn from it? What better choices would I make in the future? Who helped me?

_____
_____
_____
_____

How do I feel now that it's out of my mind and on paper?
(tick or colour in your chosen emotion and/or write it down)

_____
_____

That's great! **It's so important to acknowledge the negative, so you can release it and may learn from it.** Please move on to the yangs.

MY YANGS

What was positive about today?
What did I achieve? What made me happy?

_____

_____

_____

_____

_____

_____

_____

_____

How did it make me feel?
(tick or colour in your chosen emotion and write about it)

😄 🙂 🙂

_____

_____

_____

Excellent! **It's just as important to recognise all the positives so you can appreciate your life and see how lucky you are.** ★★

Date _____

MY YINS

What was challenging about today?
How did it make me feel?

_____

_____

_____

_____

What did I learn from it? What better choices would I make
in the future? Who helped me?

_____

_____

_____

_____

How do I feel now that it's out of my mind and on paper?
(tick or colour in your chosen emotion and/or write it down)

_____

_____

That's great! **It's so important to acknowledge the negative, so you can release it and may learn from it.** Please move on to the yangs.

MY YANGS

What was positive about today?
What did I achieve? What made me happy?

_____

_____

_____

_____

_____

_____

_____

_____

How did it make me feel?
(tick or colour in your chosen emotion and write about it)

😄 🙂 😊

_____

_____

_____

Excellent! **It's just as important to recognise all the positives so you can appreciate your life and see how lucky you are.** ⭐

Let us give thanks
for our shadows
for they are there
in the first place
because of the
presence of light.

Kamand Kojouri

FREE FLOW SPACE
(Use this page to write, draw or doodle)

Date _____

MY YINS

What was challenging about today?
How did it make me feel?

_____

_____

_____

_____

What did I learn from it? What better choices would I make in the future? Who helped me?

_____

_____

_____

_____

How do I feel now that it's out of my mind and on paper?
(tick or colour in your chosen emotion and/or write it down)

_____

That's great! **It's so important to acknowledge the negative, so you can release it and may learn from it.** Please move on to the yangs.

MY YANGS

What was positive about today?
What did I achieve? What made me happy?

_____

_____

_____

_____

_____

_____

_____

_____

_____

_____

How did it make me feel?
(tick or colour in your chosen emotion and write about it)

😄 🙂 🙂

_____

_____

_____

_____

Excellent! **It's just as important to recognise all the positives so you can appreciate your life and see how lucky you are.** ★★

Date _____

MY YINS

What was challenging about today?
How did it make me feel?

_____

_____

_____

_____

_____

What did I learn from it? What better choices would I make in the future? Who helped me?

_____

_____

_____

_____

How do I feel now that it's out of my mind and on paper?
(tick or colour in your chosen emotion and/or write it down)

_____

That's great! **It's so important to acknowledge the negative, so you can release it and may learn from it.** Please move on to the yangs.

MY YANGS

What was positive about today?
What did I achieve? What made me happy?

_____

_____

_____

_____

_____

_____

_____

_____

_____

How did it make me feel?
(tick or colour in your chosen emotion and write about it)

_____

_____

_____

Excellent! **It's just as important to recognise all the positives so you can appreciate your life and see how lucky you are.** ⭐⭐

Date

MY YINS

What was challenging about today?
How did it make me feel?

What did I learn from it? What better choices would I make in the future? Who helped me?

How do I feel now that it's out of my mind and on paper?
(tick or colour in your chosen emotion and/or write it down)

That's great! **It's so important to acknowledge the negative, so you can release it and may learn from it.** Please move on to the yangs.

MY YANGS

What was positive about today?
What did I achieve? What made me happy?

_____

_____

_____

_____

_____

_____

_____

_____

_____

_____

How did it make me feel?
(tick or colour in your chosen emotion and write about it)

_____

_____

_____

_____

Excellent! **It's just as important to recognise all the positives so you can appreciate your life and see how lucky you are.** ⭐⭐

Date _____

MY YINS

What was challenging about today?
How did it make me feel?

_____

_____

_____

_____

_____

What did I learn from it? What better choices would I make in the future? Who helped me?

_____

_____

_____

_____

_____

How do I feel now that it's out of my mind and on paper?
(tick or colour in your chosen emotion and/or write it down)

_____

_____

That's great! **It's so important to acknowledge the negative, so you can release it and may learn from it.** Please move on to the yangs.

MY YANGS

What was positive about today?
What did I achieve? What made me happy?

How did it make me feel?
(tick or colour in your chosen emotion and write about it)

Excellent! **It's just as important to recognise all the positives so you can appreciate your life and see how lucky you are.** ⭐⭐

Date ....

MY YIПS

What was challenging about today?
How did it make me feel?

_____

_____

_____

_____

_____

What did I learn from it? What better choices would I make in the future? Who helped me?

_____

_____

_____

_____

How do I feel now that it's out of my mind and on paper?
(tick or colour in your chosen emotion and/or write it down)

_____

_____

That's great! **It's so important to acknowledge the negative, so you can release it and may learn from it.** Please move on to the yangs.

MY YANGS

What was positive about today?
What did I achieve? What made me happy?

_____

_____

_____

_____

_____

_____

_____

_____

How did it make me feel?
(tick or colour in your chosen emotion and write about it)

☺ ☺ ☺

_____

_____

_____

_____

Excellent! **It's just as important to recognise all the positives so you can appreciate your life and see how lucky you are.** ★

Date _____

MY YINS

What was challenging about today?
How did it make me feel?

_____

_____

_____

_____

_____

What did I learn from it? What better choices would I make in the future? Who helped me?

_____

_____

_____

_____

How do I feel now that it's out of my mind and on paper?
(tick or colour in your chosen emotion and/or write it down)

_____

That's great! **It's so important to acknowledge the negative, so you can release it and may learn from it.** Please move on to the yangs.

MY YANGS

What was positive about today?
What did I achieve? What made me happy?

_____

_____

_____

_____

_____

_____

_____

_____

_____

How did it make me feel?
(tick or colour in your chosen emotion and write about it)

☺ ☺ ☺

_____

_____

_____

Excellent! **It's just as important to recognise all the positives so you can appreciate your life and see how lucky you are.** ✯★

Date _____

MY YINS

What was challenging about today?
How did it make me feel?

_____

_____

_____

_____

_____

What did I learn from it? What better choices would I make in the future? Who helped me?

_____

_____

_____

_____

How do I feel now that it's out of my mind and on paper?
(tick or colour in your chosen emotion and/or write it down)

_____

That's great! **It's so important to acknowledge the negative, so you can release it and may learn from it.** Please move on to the yangs.

MY YANGS

What was positive about today?
What did I achieve? What made me happy?

_____
_____
_____
_____
_____
_____
_____
_____
_____
_____

How did it make me feel?
(tick or colour in your chosen emotion and write about it)

☺ ☺ ☺

_____
_____
_____

Excellent! **It's just as important to recognise all the positives so you can appreciate your life and see how lucky you are.** ★★

Pain and pleasure are
the yin and yang of love.

J. Earp

FREE FLOW SPACE
(use this page to write, draw or doodle)

Date _____

MY YINS

What was challenging about today?
How did it make me feel?

_____

_____

_____

_____

_____

What did I learn from it? What better choices would I make in the future? Who helped me?

_____

_____

_____

_____

How do I feel now that it's out of my mind and on paper?
(tick or colour in your chosen emotion and/or write it down)

_____

_____

That's great! **It's so important to acknowledge the negative, so you can release it and may learn from it.** Please move on to the yangs.

MY YANGS

What was positive about today?
What did I achieve? What made me happy?

_____

_____

_____

_____

_____

_____

_____

_____

_____

_____

How did it make me feel?
(tick or colour in your chosen emotion and write about it)

_____

_____

_____

_____

Excellent! **It's just as important to recognise all the positives so you can appreciate your life and see how lucky you are.** ⭐⭐

Date _____

MY YINS

What was challenging about today?
How did it make me feel?

_____

_____

_____

_____

_____

What did I learn from it? What better choices would I make in the future? Who helped me?

_____

_____

_____

_____

How do I feel now that it's out of my mind and on paper?
(tick or colour in your chosen emotion and/or write it down)

_____

_____

That's great! **It's so important to acknowledge the negative, so you can release it and may learn from it.** Please move on to the yangs.

MY YANGS

What was positive about today?
What did I achieve? What made me happy?

_____

_____

_____

_____

_____

_____

_____

_____

_____

How did it make me feel?
(tick or colour in your chosen emotion and write about it)

_____

_____

_____

_____

Excellent! **It's just as important to recognise all the positives so you can appreciate your life and see how lucky you are.** ⭐

Date _____

MY YINS

What was challenging about today?
How did it make me feel?

_____

_____

_____

_____

What did I learn from it? What better choices would I make
in the future? Who helped me?

_____

_____

_____

_____

How do I feel now that it's out of my mind and on paper?
(tick or colour in your chosen emotion and/or write it down)

_____

_____

That's great! **It's so important to acknowledge the negative, so you can release it and may learn from it.** Please move on to the yangs.

MY YANGS

What was positive about today?
What did I achieve? What made me happy?

_____

_____

_____

_____

_____

_____

_____

_____

How did it make me feel?
(tick or colour in your chosen emotion and write about it)

☺ ☺ ☺

_____

_____

_____

_____

Excellent! **It's just as important to recognise all the positives so you can appreciate your life and see how lucky you are.** ✰✰

Date ....

MY YINS

What was challenging about today?
How did it make me feel?

....

....

....

....

....

What did I learn from it? What better choices would I make in the future? Who helped me?

....

....

....

....

How do I feel now that it's out of my mind and on paper?
(tick or colour in your chosen emotion and/or write it down)

....

....

That's great! **It's so important to acknowledge the negative, so you can release it and may learn from it.** Please move on to the yangs.

MY YANGS

What was positive about today?
What did I achieve? What made me happy?

_____

_____

_____

_____

_____

_____

_____

_____

How did it make me feel?
(tick or colour in your chosen emotion and write about it)

☺ ☺ ☺

_____

_____

_____

Excellent! It's just as important to recognise all the positives so you can appreciate your life and see how lucky you are. ★★

Date _____

MY YINS

What was challenging about today?
How did it make me feel?

_____

_____

_____

_____

_____

What did I learn from it? What better choices would I make in the future? Who helped me?

_____

_____

_____

_____

How do I feel now that it's out of my mind and on paper?
(tick or colour in your chosen emotion and/or write it down)

_____

_____

That's great! **It's so important to acknowledge the negative, so you can release it and may learn from it.** Please move on to the yangs.

MY YANGS

What was positive about today?
What did I achieve? What made me happy?

_____

_____

_____

_____

_____

_____

_____

_____

How did it make me feel?
(tick or colour in your chosen emotion and write about it)

😄 🙂 😊

_____

_____

_____

_____

Excellent! **It's just as important to recognise all the positives so you can appreciate your life and see how lucky you are.** ⭐

Date _____

MY YINS

What was challenging about today?
How did it make me feel?

_____

_____

_____

_____

_____

What did I learn from it? What better choices would I make in the future? Who helped me?

_____

_____

_____

_____

How do I feel now that it's out of my mind and on paper?
(tick or colour in your chosen emotion and/or write it down)

_____

That's great! **It's so important to acknowledge the negative, so you can release it and may learn from it.** Please move on to the yangs.

MY YANGS

What was positive about today?
What did I achieve? What made me happy?

_____

_____

_____

_____

_____

_____

_____

_____

How did it make me feel?
(tick or colour in your chosen emotion and write about it)

_____

_____

_____

Excellent! **It's just as important to recognise all the positives so you can appreciate your life and see how lucky you are.** ✯✦

Date

MY YINS

What was challenging about today?
How did it make me feel?

What did I learn from it? What better choices would I make in the future? Who helped me?

How do I feel now that it's out of my mind and on paper?
(tick or colour in your chosen emotion and/or write it down)

That's great! **It's so important to acknowledge the negative, so you can release it and may learn from it.** Please move on to the yangs.

MY YANGS

What was positive about today?
What did I achieve? What made me happy?

_____

_____

_____

_____

_____

_____

_____

_____

_____

_____

How did it make me feel?
(tick or colour in your chosen emotion and write about it)

_____

_____

_____

_____

Excellent! **It's just as important to recognise all the positives so you can appreciate your life and see how lucky you are.** ⭐

Freedom without discipline is foolish, discipline without freedom is insanity.

Ilona Mialik

FREE FLOW SPACE
(Use this page to write, draw or doodle)

Date ....

MY YINS

What was challenging about today?
How did it make me feel?

....
....
....
....

What did I learn from it? What better choices would I make in the future? Who helped me?

....
....
....
....

How do I feel now that it's out of my mind and on paper?
(tick or colour in your chosen emotion and/or write it down)

....

That's great! **It's so important to acknowledge the negative, so you can release it and may learn from it.** Please move on to the yangs.

MY YANGS

What was positive about today?
What did I achieve? What made me happy?

_____

_____

_____

_____

_____

_____

_____

_____

_____

How did it make me feel?
(tick or colour in your chosen emotion and write about it)

_____

_____

_____

_____

Excellent! **It's just as important to recognise all the positives so you can appreciate your life and see how lucky you are.** ⭐⭐

Date _____

MY YINS

What was challenging about today?
How did it make me feel?

_____

_____

_____

_____

What did I learn from it? What better choices would I make in the future? Who helped me?

_____

_____

_____

_____

How do I feel now that it's out of my mind and on paper?
(tick or colour in your chosen emotion and/or write it down)

_____

That's great! **It's so important to acknowledge the negative, so you can release it and may learn from it.** Please move on to the yangs.

MY YANGS

What was positive about today?
What did I achieve? What made me happy?

_____

_____

_____

_____

_____

_____

_____

_____

_____

How did it make me feel?
(tick or colour in your chosen emotion and write about it)

_____

_____

_____

_____

Excellent! **It's just as important to recognise all the positives so you can appreciate your life and see how lucky you are.** ⭐⭐

Date ....

MY YINS

What was challenging about today?
How did it make me feel?

....

....

....

....

What did I learn from it? What better choices would I make in the future? Who helped me?

....

....

....

....

How do I feel now that it's out of my mind and on paper?
(tick or colour in your chosen emotion and/or write it down)

....

....

That's great! **It's so important to acknowledge the negative, so you can release it and may learn from it.** Please move on to the yangs.

MY YANGS

What was positive about today?
What did I achieve? What made me happy?

_____

_____

_____

_____

_____

_____

_____

How did it make me feel?
(tick or colour in your chosen emotion and write about it)

☺ ☺ ☺

_____

_____

_____

_____

Excellent! **It's just as important to recognise all the positives so you can appreciate your life and see how lucky you are.** ★⋆

Date

MY YINS

What was challenging about today?
How did it make me feel?

What did I learn from it? What better choices would I make in the future? Who helped me?

How do I feel now that it's out of my mind and on paper?
(tick or colour in your chosen emotion and/or write it down)

That's great! **It's so important to acknowledge the negative, so you can release it and may learn from it.** Please move on to the yangs.

MY YANGS

What was positive about today?
What did I achieve? What made me happy?

_____

_____

_____

_____

_____

_____

_____

_____

_____

How did it make me feel?
(tick or colour in your chosen emotion and write about it)

_____

_____

_____

_____

Excellent! **It's just as important to recognise all the positives so you can appreciate your life and see how lucky you are.** ⭐

Date _____

MY YINS

What was challenging about today?
How did it make me feel?

_____

_____

_____

_____

What did I learn from it? What better choices would I make in the future? Who helped me?

_____

_____

_____

_____

How do I feel now that it's out of my mind and on paper?
(tick or colour in your chosen emotion and/or write it down)

_____

That's great! **It's so important to acknowledge the negative, so you can release it and may learn from it.** Please move on to the yangs.

MY YANGS

What was positive about today?
What did I achieve? What made me happy?

_____

_____

_____

_____

_____

_____

_____

_____

_____

How did it make me feel?
(tick or colour in your chosen emotion and write about it)

_____

_____

_____

_____

Excellent! **It's just as important to recognise all the positives so you can appreciate your life and see how lucky you are.** ⭐

Date _____

MY YINS

What was challenging about today?
How did it make me feel?

_____

_____

_____

_____

_____

What did I learn from it? What better choices would I make in the future? Who helped me?

_____

_____

_____

_____

How do I feel now that it's out of my mind and on paper?
(tick or colour in your chosen emotion and/or write it down)

_____

That's great! **It's so important to acknowledge the negative, so you can release it and may learn from it.** Please move on to the yangs.

MY YANGS

What was positive about today?
What did I achieve? What made me happy?

_____

_____

_____

_____

_____

_____

_____

_____

_____

How did it make me feel?
(tick or colour in your chosen emotion and write about it)

😄 🙂 😊

_____

_____

_____

Excellent! **It's just as important to recognise all the positives so you can appreciate your life and see how lucky you are.** ★⋆

Date ....

MY YINS

What was challenging about today?
How did it make me feel?

_____

_____

_____

_____

_____

What did I learn from it? What better choices would I make in the future? Who helped me?

_____

_____

_____

_____

How do I feel now that it's out of my mind and on paper?
(tick or colour in your chosen emotion and/or write it down)

_____

_____

That's great! **It's so important to acknowledge the negative, so you can release it and may learn from it.** Please move on to the yangs.

MY YANGS

What was positive about today?
What did I achieve? What made me happy?

How did it make me feel?
(tick or colour in your chosen emotion and write about it)

😄 🙂 😊

Excellent! **It's just as important to recognise all the positives so you can appreciate your life and see how lucky you are.** ★★

Remember the balance;
the give-and-take of
energy. The symbol of yin
and yang is more than
the integration of male
and female. It's also the
balance of light and dark,
soft and hard, active and
passive, in and out, giver
and receiver. You can't
have one without
the other.

Brownell Landrum

FREE FLOW SPACE
(Use this page to write, draw or doodle)

Date _____

MY YINS

What was challenging about today?
How did it make me feel?

_____
_____
_____
_____
_____

What did I learn from it? What better choices would I make in the future? Who helped me?

_____
_____
_____
_____

How do I feel now that it's out of my mind and on paper?
(tick or colour in your chosen emotion and/or write it down)

_____
_____

That's great! **It's so important to acknowledge the negative, so you can release it and may learn from it.** Please move on to the yangs.

MY YANGS

What was positive about today?
What did I achieve? What made me happy?

_____

_____

_____

_____

_____

_____

_____

_____

_____

How did it make me feel?
(tick or colour in your chosen emotion and write about it)

☺ ☺ ☺

_____

_____

_____

Excellent! **It's just as important to recognise all the positives so you can appreciate your life and see how lucky you are.** ✮★

Date _____

MY YINS

What was challenging about today?
How did it make me feel?

_____

_____

_____

_____

_____

What did I learn from it? What better choices would I make in the future? Who helped me?

_____

_____

_____

_____

How do I feel now that it's out of my mind and on paper?
(tick or colour in your chosen emotion and/or write it down)

_____

_____

That's great! **It's so important to acknowledge the negative, so you can release it and may learn from it.** Please move on to the yangs.

MY YANGS

What was positive about today?
What did I achieve? What made me happy?

_____

_____

_____

_____

_____

_____

_____

_____

_____

How did it make me feel?
(tick or colour in your chosen emotion and write about it)

😄 ☺ 🙂

_____

_____

_____

Excellent! **It's just as important to recognise all the positives so you can appreciate your life and see how lucky you are.** ✰⋆

Date _____

MY YIN5

What was challenging about today?
How did it make me feel?

_____

_____

_____

_____

_____

_____

What did I learn from it? What better choices would I make in the future? Who helped me?

_____

_____

_____

_____

How do I feel now that it's out of my mind and on paper?
(tick or colour in your chosen emotion and/or write it down)

_____

_____

That's great! **It's so important to acknowledge the negative, so you can release it and may learn from it.** Please move on to the yangs.

MY YANGS

What was positive about today?
What did I achieve? What made me happy?

_____

_____

_____

_____

_____

_____

_____

_____

_____

How did it make me feel?
(tick or colour in your chosen emotion and write about it)

☺ ☺ ☺

_____

_____

_____

Excellent! **It's just as important to recognise all the positives so you can appreciate your life and see how lucky you are.** ✯⋆

Date _____

MY YINS

What was challenging about today?
How did it make me feel?

_____

_____

_____

_____

_____

What did I learn from it? What better choices would I make
in the future? Who helped me?

_____

_____

_____

_____

How do I feel now that it's out of my mind and on paper?
(tick or colour in your chosen emotion and/or write it down)

_____

_____

That's great! **It's so important to acknowledge the negative, so you can release it and may learn from it.** Please move on to the yangs.

MY YANGS

What was positive about today?
What did I achieve? What made me happy?

_____

_____

_____

_____

_____

_____

_____

_____

How did it make me feel?
(tick or colour in your chosen emotion and write about it)

_____

_____

_____

_____

Excellent! **It's just as important to recognise all the positives so you can appreciate your life and see how lucky you are.**

Date _____

MY YINS

What was challenging about today?
How did it make me feel?

_____

_____

_____

_____

_____

What did I learn from it? What better choices would I make in the future? Who helped me?

_____

_____

_____

_____

How do I feel now that it's out of my mind and on paper?
(tick or colour in your chosen emotion and/or write it down)

_____

_____

That's great! **It's so important to acknowledge the negative, so you can release it and may learn from it.** Please move on to the yangs.

MY YANGS

What was positive about today?
What did I achieve? What made me happy?

_____

_____

_____

_____

_____

_____

_____

_____

_____

_____

How did it make me feel?
(tick or colour in your chosen emotion and write about it)

_____

_____

_____

_____

Excellent! **It's just as important to recognise all the positives so you can appreciate your life and see how lucky you are.** ✯✦

Date

MY YINS

What was challenging about today?
How did it make me feel?

What did I learn from it? What better choices would I make
in the future? Who helped me?

How do I feel now that it's out of my mind and on paper?
(tick or colour in your chosen emotion and/or write it down)

That's great! **It's so important to acknowledge the negative, so you can release it and may learn from it.** Please move on to the yangs.

MY YANGS

What was positive about today?
What did I achieve? What made me happy?

_____

_____

_____

_____

_____

_____

_____

_____

_____

How did it make me feel?
(tick or colour in your chosen emotion and write about it)

😄　　🙂　　☺️

_____

_____

_____

Excellent! **It's just as important to recognise all the positives so you can appreciate your life and see how lucky you are.** ⭐

Date _____

MY YINS

What was challenging about today?
How did it make me feel?

_____

_____

_____

_____

_____

What did I learn from it? What better choices would I make in the future? Who helped me?

_____

_____

_____

_____

How do I feel now that it's out of my mind and on paper?
(tick or colour in your chosen emotion and/or write it down)

_____

_____

That's great! **It's so important to acknowledge the negative, so you can release it and may learn from it.** Please move on to the yangs.

MY YANGS

What was positive about today?
What did I achieve? What made me happy?

_____

_____

_____

_____

_____

_____

_____

_____

_____

How did it make me feel?
(tick or colour in your chosen emotion and write about it)

😄　🙂　😊

_____

_____

_____

Excellent! **It's just as important to recognise all the positives so you can appreciate your life and see how lucky you are.** ⭐★

The world is, was, will
always be filled with
good and evil, because
good and evil is the
yin and yang of the
human condition.

Philip Zimbardo

FREE FLOW SPACE
(Use this page to write, draw or doodle)

Date _____

MY YINS

What was challenging about today?
How did it make me feel?

_____

_____

_____

_____

_____

What did I learn from it? What better choices would I make in the future? Who helped me?

_____

_____

_____

_____

How do I feel now that it's out of my mind and on paper?
(tick or colour in your chosen emotion and/or write it down)

_____

_____

That's great! **It's so important to acknowledge the negative, so you can release it and may learn from it.** Please move on to the yangs.

MY YANGS

What was positive about today?
What did I achieve? What made me happy?

_____

_____

_____

_____

_____

_____

_____

_____

_____

How did it make me feel?
(tick or colour in your chosen emotion and write about it)

_____

_____

_____

_____

Excellent! **It's just as important to recognise all the positives so you can appreciate your life and see how lucky you are.** ★★

Date

MY YINS

What was challenging about today?
How did it make me feel?

What did I learn from it? What better choices would I make
in the future? Who helped me?

How do I feel now that it's out of my mind and on paper?
(tick or colour in your chosen emotion and/or write it down)

That's great! **It's so important to acknowledge the negative, so you
can release it and may learn from it.** Please move on to the yangs.

MY YANGS

What was positive about today?
What did I achieve? What made me happy?

_____

_____

_____

_____

_____

_____

_____

_____

How did it make me feel?
(tick or colour in your chosen emotion and write about it)

😄 ☺ 😊

_____

_____

_____

Excellent! **It's just as important to recognise all the positives so you can appreciate your life and see how lucky you are.** ✯✫

Date

MY YINS

What was challenging about today?
How did it make me feel?

_____

_____

_____

_____

_____

What did I learn from it? What better choices would I make
in the future? Who helped me?

_____

_____

_____

_____

How do I feel now that it's out of my mind and on paper?
(tick or colour in your chosen emotion and/or write it down)

_____

_____

That's great! **It's so important to acknowledge the negative, so you
can release it and may learn from it.** Please move on to the yangs.

MY YANGS

What was positive about today?
What did I achieve? What made me happy?

_____

_____

_____

_____

_____

_____

_____

_____

_____

How did it make me feel?
(tick or colour in your chosen emotion and write about it)

_____

_____

_____

Excellent! **It's just as important to recognise all the positives so you can appreciate your life and see how lucky you are.** ⭐

Date

MY YINS

What was challenging about today?
How did it make me feel?

What did I learn from it? What better choices would I make in the future? Who helped me?

How do I feel now that it's out of my mind and on paper?
(tick or colour in your chosen emotion and/or write it down)

That's great! **It's so important to acknowledge the negative, so you can release it and may learn from it.** Please move on to the yangs.

MY YANGS

What was positive about today?
What did I achieve? What made me happy?

_____

_____

_____

_____

_____

_____

_____

_____

_____

How did it make me feel?
(tick or colour in your chosen emotion and write about it)

😄 🙂 🙂

_____

_____

_____

_____

Excellent! **It's just as important to recognise all the positives so you can appreciate your life and see how lucky you are.** ⭐

Date ....

MY YINS

What was challenging about today?
How did it make me feel?

....

....

....

....

....

What did I learn from it? What better choices would I make in the future? Who helped me?

....

....

....

....

How do I feel now that it's out of my mind and on paper?
(tick or colour in your chosen emotion and/or write it down)

....

....

That's great! **It's so important to acknowledge the negative, so you can release it and may learn from it.** Please move on to the yangs.

MY YANGS

What was positive about today?
What did I achieve? What made me happy?

_____

_____

_____

_____

_____

_____

_____

_____

_____

_____

How did it make me feel?
(tick or colour in your chosen emotion and write about it)

_____

_____

_____

Excellent! **It's just as important to recognise all the positives so you can appreciate your life and see how lucky you are.** ★★

Date ....

MY YINS

What was challenging about today?
How did it make me feel?

....

....

....

....

What did I learn from it? What better choices would I make in the future? Who helped me?

....

....

....

....

How do I feel now that it's out of my mind and on paper?
(tick or colour in your chosen emotion and/or write it down)

....

....

That's great! **It's so important to acknowledge the negative, so you can release it and may learn from it.** Please move on to the yangs.

MY YANGS

What was positive about today?
What did I achieve? What made me happy?

_____

_____

_____

_____

_____

_____

_____

_____

_____

How did it make me feel?
(tick or colour in your chosen emotion and write about it)

😄 🙂 😊

_____

_____

_____

Excellent! **It's just as important to recognise all the positives so you can appreciate your life and see how lucky you are.** ⭐

Date _____

MY YIПS

What was challenging about today?
How did it make me feel?

_____

_____

_____

_____

_____

What did I learn from it? What better choices would I make
in the future? Who helped me?

_____

_____

_____

_____

How do I feel now that it's out of my mind and on paper?
(tick or colour in your chosen emotion and/or write it down)

_____

_____

That's great! **It's so important to acknowledge the negative, so you can release it and may learn from it.** Please move on to the yangs.

MY YANGS

What was positive about today?
What did I achieve? What made me happy?

_____

_____

_____

_____

_____

_____

_____

_____

How did it make me feel?
(tick or colour in your chosen emotion and write about it)

😄 🙂 😊

_____

_____

_____

Excellent! **It's just as important to recognise all the positives so you can appreciate your life and see how lucky you are.** ⭐★

Your greatest attribute, that which allows you to accomplish most in life and the most treasured aspect of your being will often be the source of your greatest suffering.

Chris Matakas

FREE FLOW SPACE
(Use this page to write, draw or doodle)

Date _____

MY YINS

What was challenging about today?
How did it make me feel?

_____

_____

_____

_____

_____

What did I learn from it? What better choices would I make in the future? Who helped me?

_____

_____

_____

_____

How do I feel now that it's out of my mind and on paper?
(tick or colour in your chosen emotion and/or write it down)

_____

_____

That's great! **It's so important to acknowledge the negative, so you can release it and may learn from it.** Please move on to the yangs.

MY YANGS

What was positive about today?
What did I achieve? What made me happy?

_____

_____

_____

_____

_____

_____

_____

_____

_____

_____

How did it make me feel?
(tick or colour in your chosen emotion and write about it)

😄 ☺ 🙂

_____

_____

_____

Excellent! **It's just as important to recognise all the positives so you can appreciate your life and see how lucky you are.** ★✦

Date _____

MY YINS

What was challenging about today?
How did it make me feel?

_____

_____

_____

_____

_____

What did I learn from it? What better choices would I make
in the future? Who helped me?

_____

_____

_____

_____

How do I feel now that it's out of my mind and on paper?
(tick or colour in your chosen emotion and/or write it down)

_____

_____

That's great! **It's so important to acknowledge the negative, so you
can release it and may learn from it.** Please move on to the yangs.

MY YANGS

What was positive about today?
What did I achieve? What made me happy?

_____

_____

_____

_____

_____

_____

_____

_____

_____

_____

_____

_____

How did it make me feel?
(tick or colour in your chosen emotion and write about it)

☺ ☺ ☺

_____

_____

_____

Excellent! **It's just as important to recognise all the positives so you can appreciate your life and see how lucky you are.** ✯★

Date _____

MY YINS

What was challenging about today?
How did it make me feel?

_____

_____

_____

_____

_____

What did I learn from it? What better choices would I make in the future? Who helped me?

_____

_____

_____

_____

How do I feel now that it's out of my mind and on paper?
(tick or colour in your chosen emotion and/or write it down)

_____

_____

That's great! **It's so important to acknowledge the negative, so you can release it and may learn from it.** Please move on to the yangs.

MY YANGS

What was positive about today?
What did I achieve? What made me happy?

How did it make me feel?
(tick or colour in your chosen emotion and write about it)

Excellent! **It's just as important to recognise all the positives so you can appreciate your life and see how lucky you are.** ⭐

Date _____

MY YINS

What was challenging about today?
How did it make me feel?

_____

_____

_____

_____

What did I learn from it? What better choices would I make in the future? Who helped me?

_____

_____

_____

_____

How do I feel now that it's out of my mind and on paper?
(tick or colour in your chosen emotion and/or write it down)

_____

_____

That's great! **It's so important to acknowledge the negative, so you can release it and may learn from it.** Please move on to the yangs.

MY YANGS

What was positive about today?
What did I achieve? What made me happy?

_____

_____

_____

_____

_____

_____

_____

_____

_____

_____

How did it make me feel?
(tick or colour in your chosen emotion and write about it)

_____

_____

_____

Excellent! **It's just as important to recognise all the positives so you can appreciate your life and see how lucky you are.** ⋆

Date

MY YINS

What was challenging about today?
How did it make me feel?

What did I learn from it? What better choices would I make in the future? Who helped me?

How do I feel now that it's out of my mind and on paper?
(tick or colour in your chosen emotion and/or write it down)

That's great! **It's so important to acknowledge the negative, so you can release it and may learn from it.** Please move on to the yangs.

MY YANGS

What was positive about today?
What did I achieve? What made me happy?

_____

_____

_____

_____

_____

_____

_____

_____

_____

How did it make me feel?
(tick or colour in your chosen emotion and write about it)

_____

_____

_____

Excellent! **It's just as important to recognise all the positives so you can appreciate your life and see how lucky you are.** ★

Date _____

MY YINS

What was challenging about today?
How did it make me feel?

_____

_____

_____

_____

_____

What did I learn from it? What better choices would I make in the future? Who helped me?

_____

_____

_____

_____

How do I feel now that it's out of my mind and on paper?
(tick or colour in your chosen emotion and/or write it down)

_____

_____

That's great! **It's so important to acknowledge the negative, so you can release it and may learn from it.** Please move on to the yangs.

MY YANGS

What was positive about today?
What did I achieve? What made me happy?

How did it make me feel?
(tick or colour in your chosen emotion and write about it)

Excellent! **It's just as important to recognise all the positives so you can appreciate your life and see how lucky you are.** ⭐

Date

MY YINS

What was challenging about today?
How did it make me feel?

What did I learn from it? What better choices would I make in the future? Who helped me?

How do I feel now that it's out of my mind and on paper?
(tick or colour in your chosen emotion and/or write it down)

That's great! **It's so important to acknowledge the negative, so you can release it and may learn from it.** Please move on to the yangs.

MY YANGS

What was positive about today?
What did I achieve? What made me happy?

_____

_____

_____

_____

_____

_____

_____

_____

How did it make me feel?
(tick or colour in your chosen emotion and write about it)

_____

_____

_____

_____

Excellent! **It's just as important to recognise all the positives so you can appreciate your life and see how lucky you are.** ★★

For you are more than just a thought. You are my everything. You are my Yin as I am your Yang. Together we make the world go round.

Angelia Bailey

FREE FLOW SPACE
(Use this page to write, draw or doodle)

Date

MY YINS

What was challenging about today?
How did it make me feel?

What did I learn from it? What better choices would I make in the future? Who helped me?

How do I feel now that it's out of my mind and on paper?
(tick or colour in your chosen emotion and/or write it down)

That's great! **It's so important to acknowledge the negative, so you can release it and may learn from it.** Please move on to the yangs.

MY YANGS

What was positive about today?
What did I achieve? What made me happy?

_____

_____

_____

_____

_____

_____

_____

_____

How did it make me feel?
(tick or colour in your chosen emotion and write about it)

_____

_____

_____

Excellent! **It's just as important to recognise all the positives so you can appreciate your life and see how lucky you are.**

Date ....

MY YINS

What was challenging about today?
How did it make me feel?

What did I learn from it? What better choices would I make
in the future? Who helped me?

How do I feel now that it's out of my mind and on paper?
(tick or colour in your chosen emotion and/or write it down)

That's great! **It's so important to acknowledge the negative, so you can release it and may learn from it.** Please move on to the yangs.

MY YANGS

What was positive about today?
What did I achieve? What made me happy?

_____

_____

_____

_____

_____

_____

_____

_____

_____

How did it make me feel?
(tick or colour in your chosen emotion and write about it)

_____

_____

_____

_____

Excellent! **It's just as important to recognise all the positives so you can appreciate your life and see how lucky you are.**

Date

MY YINS

What was challenging about today?
How did it make me feel?

What did I learn from it? What better choices would I make in the future? Who helped me?

How do I feel now that it's out of my mind and on paper?
(tick or colour in your chosen emotion and/or write it down)

That's great! **It's so important to acknowledge the negative, so you can release it and may learn from it.** Please move on to the yangs.

MY YANGS

What was positive about today?
What did I achieve? What made me happy?

_____

_____

_____

_____

_____

_____

_____

_____

_____

_____

How did it make me feel?
(tick or colour in your chosen emotion and write about it)

_____

_____

_____

Excellent! **It's just as important to recognise all the positives so you can appreciate your life and see how lucky you are.** ★★

Date

MY YINS

What was challenging about today?
How did it make me feel?

What did I learn from it? What better choices would I make in the future? Who helped me?

How do I feel now that it's out of my mind and on paper?
(tick or colour in your chosen emotion and/or write it down)

That's great! **It's so important to acknowledge the negative, so you can release it and may learn from it.** Please move on to the yangs.

MY YANGS

What was positive about today?
What did I achieve? What made me happy?

_____
_____
_____
_____
_____
_____
_____
_____
_____
_____

How did it make me feel?
(tick or colour in your chosen emotion and write about it)

_____
_____
_____
_____

Excellent! **It's just as important to recognise all the positives so you can appreciate your life and see how lucky you are.** ⭐

Date

MY YIПS

What was challenging about today?
How did it make me feel?

What did I learn from it? What better choices would I make in the future? Who helped me?

How do I feel now that it's out of my mind and on paper?
(tick or colour in your chosen emotion and/or write it down)

That's great! **It's so important to acknowledge the negative, so you can release it and may learn from it.** Please move on to the yangs.

MY YANGS

What was positive about today?
What did I achieve? What made me happy?

_____

_____

_____

_____

_____

_____

_____

_____

_____

_____

How did it make me feel?
(tick or colour in your chosen emotion and write about it)

_____

_____

_____

Excellent! **It's just as important to recognise all the positives so you can appreciate your life and see how lucky you are.** ✯✯

Date _____

MY YINS

What was challenging about today?
How did it make me feel?

_____

_____

_____

_____

_____

What did I learn from it? What better choices would I make in the future? Who helped me?

_____

_____

_____

_____

How do I feel now that it's out of my mind and on paper?
(tick or colour in your chosen emotion and/or write it down)

_____

_____

That's great! **It's so important to acknowledge the negative, so you can release it and may learn from it.** Please move on to the yangs.

MY YANGS

What was positive about today?
What did I achieve? What made me happy?

_____

_____

_____

_____

_____

_____

_____

_____

_____

How did it make me feel?
(tick or colour in your chosen emotion and write about it)

😄 ☺ 🙂

_____

_____

_____

Excellent! **It's just as important to recognise all the positives so you can appreciate your life and see how lucky you are.** ✦✦

Date ....

MY YINS

What was challenging about today?
How did it make me feel?

_____

_____

_____

_____

_____

What did I learn from it? What better choices would I make in the future? Who helped me?

_____

_____

_____

_____

How do I feel now that it's out of my mind and on paper?
(tick or colour in your chosen emotion and/or write it down)

_____

_____

That's great! **It's so important to acknowledge the negative, so you can release it and may learn from it.** Please move on to the yangs.

MY YANGS

What was positive about today?
What did I achieve? What made me happy?

How did it make me feel?
(tick or colour in your chosen emotion and write about it)

Excellent! **It's just as important to recognise all the positives so you can appreciate your life and see how lucky you are.** ⭐⭐

We are only different because there exists something to be different from, and it is this difference that bonds us.

Chris Matakas

FREE FLOW SPACE
(Use this page to write, draw or doodle)

Date ....

MY YINS

What was challenging about today?
How did it make me feel?

....
....
....
....

What did I learn from it? What better choices would I make in the future? Who helped me?

....
....
....
....

How do I feel now that it's out of my mind and on paper?
(tick or colour in your chosen emotion and/or write it down)

....
....

That's great! **It's so important to acknowledge the negative, so you can release it and may learn from it.** Please move on to the yangs.

MY YANGS

What was positive about today?
What did I achieve? What made me happy?

_____

_____

_____

_____

_____

_____

_____

_____

_____

How did it make me feel?
(tick or colour in your chosen emotion and write about it)

😄 🙂 😊

_____

_____

_____

Excellent! **It's just as important to recognise all the positives so you can appreciate your life and see how lucky you are.** ★⋆

Date ....

MY YINS

What was challenging about today?
How did it make me feel?

_____

_____

_____

_____

_____

What did I learn from it? What better choices would I make
in the future? Who helped me?

_____

_____

_____

_____

How do I feel now that it's out of my mind and on paper?
(tick or colour in your chosen emotion and/or write it down)

_____

_____

That's great! **It's so important to acknowledge the negative, so you can release it and may learn from it.** Please move on to the yangs.

MY YANGS

What was positive about today?
What did I achieve? What made me happy?

_____

_____

_____

_____

_____

_____

_____

_____

_____

How did it make me feel?
(tick or colour in your chosen emotion and write about it)

_____

_____

_____

Excellent! **It's just as important to recognise all the positives so you can appreciate your life and see how lucky you are.** ★★

Date ....

MY YINS

What was challenging about today?
How did it make me feel?

....

....

....

....

What did I learn from it? What better choices would I make in the future? Who helped me?

....

....

....

....

How do I feel now that it's out of my mind and on paper?
(tick or colour in your chosen emotion and/or write it down)

....

....

That's great! **It's so important to acknowledge the negative, so you can release it and may learn from it.** Please move on to the yangs.

MY YANGS

What was positive about today?
What did I achieve? What made me happy?

_____

_____

_____

_____

_____

_____

_____

_____

_____

How did it make me feel?
(tick or colour in your chosen emotion and write about it)

😄 🙂 😊

_____

_____

_____

_____

Excellent! **It's just as important to recognise all the positives so you can appreciate your life and see how lucky you are.** ⭐⋆

Date ....

MY YINS

What was challenging about today?
How did it make me feel?

What did I learn from it? What better choices would I make in the future? Who helped me?

How do I feel now that it's out of my mind and on paper?
(tick or colour in your chosen emotion and/or write it down)

That's great! **It's so important to acknowledge the negative, so you can release it and may learn from it.** Please move on to the yangs.

MY YANGS

What was positive about today?
What did I achieve? What made me happy?

_____

_____

_____

_____

_____

_____

_____

_____

_____

_____

How did it make me feel?
(tick or colour in your chosen emotion and write about it)

_____

_____

_____

_____

Excellent! **It's just as important to recognise all the positives so you can appreciate your life and see how lucky you are.** ✪✦

Date _____

MY YINS

What was challenging about today?
How did it make me feel?

_____

_____

_____

_____

_____

What did I learn from it? What better choices would I make in the future? Who helped me?

_____

_____

_____

_____

How do I feel now that it's out of my mind and on paper?
(tick or colour in your chosen emotion and/or write it down)

_____

_____

That's great! **It's so important to acknowledge the negative, so you can release it and may learn from it.** Please move on to the yangs.

MY YANGS

What was positive about today?
What did I achieve? What made me happy?

_____

_____

_____

_____

_____

_____

_____

_____

_____

How did it make me feel?
(tick or colour in your chosen emotion and write about it)

_____

_____

_____

Excellent! **It's just as important to recognise all the positives so you can appreciate your life and see how lucky you are.** ★★

Date ....

MY YINS

What was challenging about today?
How did it make me feel?

_____

_____

_____

_____

What did I learn from it? What better choices would I make in the future? Who helped me?

_____

_____

_____

_____

How do I feel now that it's out of my mind and on paper?
(tick or colour in your chosen emotion and/or write it down)

_____

_____

That's great! **It's so important to acknowledge the negative, so you can release it and may learn from it.** Please move on to the yangs.

MY YANGS

What was positive about today?
What did I achieve? What made me happy?

_____

_____

_____

_____

_____

_____

_____

_____

How did it make me feel?
(tick or colour in your chosen emotion and write about it)

😄　😊　🙂

_____

_____

_____

Excellent! **It's just as important to recognise all the positives so you can appreciate your life and see how lucky you are.** ✦

Date

MY YINS

What was challenging about today?
How did it make me feel?

What did I learn from it? What better choices would I make in the future? Who helped me?

How do I feel now that it's out of my mind and on paper?
(tick or colour in your chosen emotion and/or write it down)

That's great! **It's so important to acknowledge the negative, so you can release it and may learn from it.** Please move on to the yangs.

MY YANGS

What was positive about today?
What did I achieve? What made me happy?

How did it make me feel?
(tick or colour in your chosen emotion and write about it)

Excellent! **It's just as important to recognise all the positives so you can appreciate your life and see how lucky you are.** ★⋆

The heart of a human
being is no different
from the soul of
heaven and earth.
In your practice always
keep in your thoughts
the interaction of
heaven and earth,
water and fire,
yin and yang.

Morihei Ueshiba

FREE FLOW SPACE
(Use this page to write, draw or doodle)

Date

MY YINS

What was challenging about today?
How did it make me feel?

What did I learn from it? What better choices would I make in the future? Who helped me?

How do I feel now that it's out of my mind and on paper?
(tick or colour in your chosen emotion and/or write it down)

That's great! **It's so important to acknowledge the negative, so you can release it and may learn from it.** Please move on to the yangs.

MY YANGS

What was positive about today?
What did I achieve? What made me happy?

How did it make me feel?
(tick or colour in your chosen emotion and write about it)

Excellent! **It's just as important to recognise all the positives so you can appreciate your life and see how lucky you are.** ⭐

Date

MY YINS

What was challenging about today?
How did it make me feel?

What did I learn from it? What better choices would I make in the future? Who helped me?

How do I feel now that it's out of my mind and on paper?
(tick or colour in your chosen emotion and/or write it down)

That's great! **It's so important to acknowledge the negative, so you can release it and may learn from it.** Please move on to the yangs.

MY YANGS

What was positive about today?
What did I achieve? What made me happy?

_____

_____

_____

_____

_____

_____

_____

How did it make me feel?
(tick or colour in your chosen emotion and write about it)

😄 🙂 😊

_____

_____

_____

Excellent! **It's just as important to recognise all the positives so you can appreciate your life and see how lucky you are.** ⭐

Date

MY YINS

What was challenging about today?
How did it make me feel?

What did I learn from it? What better choices would I make in the future? Who helped me?

How do I feel now that it's out of my mind and on paper?
(tick or colour in your chosen emotion and/or write it down)

That's great! **It's so important to acknowledge the negative, so you can release it and may learn from it.** Please move on to the yangs.

MY YANGS

What was positive about today?
What did I achieve? What made me happy?

How did it make me feel?
(tick or colour in your chosen emotion and write about it)

Excellent! **It's just as important to recognise all the positives so you can appreciate your life and see how lucky you are.** ⭐⭐

Date

MY YINS

What was challenging about today?
How did it make me feel?

What did I learn from it? What better choices would I make in the future? Who helped me?

How do I feel now that it's out of my mind and on paper?
(tick or colour in your chosen emotion and/or write it down)

That's great! **It's so important to acknowledge the negative, so you can release it and may learn from it.** Please move on to the yangs.

MY YANGS

What was positive about today?
What did I achieve? What made me happy?

_____
_____
_____
_____
_____
_____
_____
_____
_____
_____

How did it make me feel?
(tick or colour in your chosen emotion and write about it)

_____
_____
_____
_____

Excellent! **It's just as important to recognise all the positives so you can appreciate your life and see how lucky you are.**

Date _____

MY YINS

What was challenging about today?
How did it make me feel?

_____

_____

_____

_____

_____

What did I learn from it? What better choices would I make in the future? Who helped me?

_____

_____

_____

_____

How do I feel now that it's out of my mind and on paper?
(tick or colour in your chosen emotion and/or write it down)

_____

_____

That's great! **It's so important to acknowledge the negative, so you can release it and may learn from it.** Please move on to the yangs.

MY YANGS

What was positive about today?
What did I achieve? What made me happy?

_____
_____
_____
_____
_____
_____
_____
_____
_____

How did it make me feel?
(tick or colour in your chosen emotion and write about it)

😄 🙂 😊

_____
_____
_____

Excellent! **It's just as important to recognise all the positives so you can appreciate your life and see how lucky you are.** ⭐

Date ....

MY YINS

What was challenging about today?
How did it make me feel?

_____

_____

_____

_____

What did I learn from it? What better choices would I make
in the future? Who helped me?

_____

_____

_____

_____

How do I feel now that it's out of my mind and on paper?
(tick or colour in your chosen emotion and/or write it down)

_____

_____

That's great! **It's so important to acknowledge the negative, so you can release it and may learn from it.** Please move on to the yangs.

MY YANGS

What was positive about today?
What did I achieve? What made me happy?

How did it make me feel?
(tick or colour in your chosen emotion and write about it)

Excellent! It's just as important to recognise all the positives so you
can appreciate your life and see how lucky you are. ⭐

Date _____

MY YINS

What was challenging about today?
How did it make me feel?

_____

_____

_____

_____

_____

What did I learn from it? What better choices would I make in the future? Who helped me?

_____

_____

_____

_____

How do I feel now that it's out of my mind and on paper?
(tick or colour in your chosen emotion and/or write it down)

_____

_____

That's great! **It's so important to acknowledge the negative, so you can release it and may learn from it.** Please move on to the yangs.

MY YANGS

What was positive about today?
What did I achieve? What made me happy?

How did it make me feel?
(tick or colour in your chosen emotion and write about it)

Excellent! **It's just as important to recognise all the positives so you can appreciate your life and see how lucky you are.**

Nature is about balance.
All the world comes in
pairs - Yin and Yang,
right and wrong,
men and women;
what's pleasure
without pain?

Angelina Jolie

FREE FLOW SPACE
(Use this page to write, draw or doodle)

FINISH HERE...

CONGRATULATIONS ON COMPLETING THIS JOURNAL!

Date: ....

Huge shout out to you on completing these 12 weeks as it's not easy. It takes a while to form habits, but hopefully now you've learnt how to get your thoughts out of your head and down on paper.

This is a chapter completed. It's up to you whether you want to continue this journey and maybe find some extra questions to ask yourself.

Has your vision changed? Great! It's important to have something to work towards, as if we are not growing, we are dying.

So where does the next part of your journey will take you?...

Answering the following questions will help you:

1. What does my vision for my future look like NOW AFTER completing this journal?
2. What are the POSITIVE changes?
3. How do I FEEL?

CHINESE SYMBOLS
in this journal

美
Beautiful

愛
Love

喜
Happiness

德
Morality

財
Wealth

幸
Lucky

希
Hope

荣
Honour

壽
Long Life

福
Blessed

智
Wisdom

德
Virtue

和
Harmony

自由
Freedom

CHINESE WRITING PRACTICE
Have fun practising drawing the symbols on the left

Notes

Notes

Notes

Notes

Notes

Notes

THANK YOU GIFT

'THE POWER OF GRATITUDE' **FREE** EBOOK

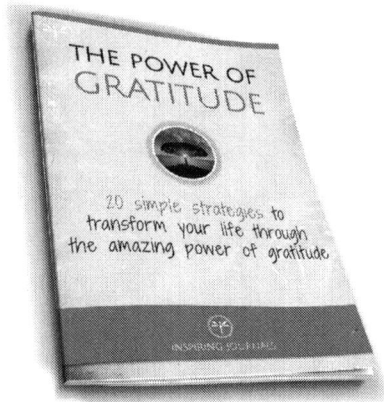

Download this beautiful 28 page eBook to discover
20 simple strategies to transform your life through
the amazing power of gratitude.

Visit **www.inspiringjournals.com/gift**

Other series and titles available:

- Love Journal
- Daily Success Journal
- Gratitude Journal Butterfly (available in 7 vibrant colours)
- Gratitude at Home Series including:
  - A parent's book 'Gratitude at Home'
  - Gratitude Journals ranging from age 2 to 20
- Gratitude in Schools Series including:
  - Teacher's guide 'Gratitude in Primary Schools'
  - Teacher's guide 'Gratitude in Secondary Schools and Further Education'
  - Gratitude Journals ranging from age 5 to 20

To find out more, visit **www.inspiringjournals.com**

33227059R00116

Printed in Great Britain
by Amazon